Test Everything:
Hold Fast to What Is Good

Test Everything:
Hold Fast to What Is Good

An Interview with

HANS URS VON BALTHASAR
by Angelo Scola

Translated by Maria Shrady

IGNATIUS PRESS   SAN FRANCISCO

Title of the German original:
Prüfet alles—das Gute behaltet
© 1986 Schwabenverlag AG, Ostfildern
Stuttgart, Germany

Cover by Victoria Hoke Lane

With ecclesiastical approval
© 1989 Ignatius Press, San Francisco
All rights reserved
ISBN 0-89870-196-1
Library of Congress catalogue number 87-80660
Printed in the United States of America

Contents

Foreword

To be interviewed by a good friend—and Don Angelo Scola certainly is such a one—is both pleasure and pain. Pleasure, because one can speak directly from the heart, touching upon one's deepest concerns, and pain, because it has to be done in such a brief and hence imprecise manner. One would like to dwell on every question, reflect on it, add nuance here or there, formulate it more intricately than it may actually emerge. But time presses on, and once again one is faced with an entirely different problem. Well, perhaps something like an image may unexpectedly arise from such a colorful mosaic. One hopes it will not be a merely subjective image of the speaker but, across the diversity of his views, an objective one of that hour now facing the Church. Much will have to be said that sounds harsh; may I be pardoned for this and may it be attributed to my shortsightedness. Or, if you will, to my age and backwardness, which show little relish for the latest novelties. Or again, to my love for a Church that has endured for two millennia, has retained her vigor throughout and thus was not born suddenly as a "post-conciliar" Church. This could be the true reason why some things may sound harsh: if one knows a bit about the history of the apostolic and holy Church, one measures them against her greatness, and then they appear in a format too flimsy for her catholicity. By holding such views, one risks being labeled "preconciliar" (as if there were such a thing) and pessimistic (which Ratzinger certainly is not; he is merely a realist). I, too, am anything but pessimistic, for the Church, assailed as she is from without and within, demonstrates by that very fact that she possesses a vitality that is unbearable for the godless world. Amidst the present din of battle, I can clearly sense this vitality, which is bursting forth with renewed life. It manifests itself in unsuspected places and in such a way that even a self-satisfied (and thus already "reactionary") mentality cannot help but acknowledge it. This new life, where, according to Goethe, the new wine often acts absurdly, must then be given an ecclesiastically acceptable form by the official Church.

Let the kind reader refrain from weighing every one of my words with a gold-scale. Let him rather pick a nugget here or there, if he comes across one.

And finally, let him bear in mind that the questions raised here are viewed from an Italian perspective, reflecting the specific interests of the Church in that country.

H. U. von Balthasar

The Church in the Modern World

Angelo Scola: In 1952, you wrote a book entitled *The Razing of the Bastions*. In it you spoke of a Church in danger of seeing herself as an entrenched fortress. What prompted you to suggest that she should raze her bastions?

Hans Urs von Balthasar: It was the realization that Jesus intended the Church to be essentially missionary in character, a community with a centrifugal movement, not a people enclosed in itself. This makes her so different from Israel, which is not a missionary but a centripetal people, adhering to itself, far more so than any other people on earth. For Israel the movement of salvation consists in the gathering of the diaspora, in the retrieving of exiles from the remote corners of the earth into the holy, ancestral land. The Church, on the other hand, lives by her mission, as expressed in the closing chapter of Saint Matthew: "Go out into the world, to all nations." That in no way contradicts her nature, which is grounded in *mysterium*, nor does it run counter to the eucharistic mystery in her midst. The Eucharist, however, may be celebrated anywhere in the world, in an African hut or in an Eskimo's igloo, and wherever it occurs is a holy land. One can point to texts in the Church Fathers where they rejoice in the fact that there exists no other holy land than the world in its totality, for Jesus, the Risen One, is everywhere present. This openness of the Church, her mystery notwithstanding, stands in contradiction to the erection of earthly "bastions" and makes the apostolic movement less believable to people who perceive this contradiction.

Perhaps I should take a look at my own past for a moment, in order to throw some light on the perspective of the fifties. The old Lucerne family into which I was born did indeed possess a liberal ancestor or two (one was even placed on the Index), but my parents were so instinctively Catholic, as if nothing more natural existed in the whole world. (And I for my part must confess that the same was true for me.) An equally serene Catholic atmosphere pervaded the colleges I attended: the Benedictines at Engelberg during the First World War, of which we students, aside from the bad cooking, were largely unaware. The same was true of the Jesuit College in Feldkirch, where my friends and I were deeply engaged in aesthetic and literary studies. I continued these studies during my university years, particularly in Zurich and Vienna and for one semester in Berlin, where I was exposed to quite different perspectives. In Vienna I became fascinated with Plotinus, and there was, of course, the inevitable encounter with depth-psychology and the Freudian circles. I found myself intensely moved by the impassioned pantheism of Mahler; Nietzsche, Hofmannsthal and George entered my vision, as did the doomsday pessimism of Karl Kraus—the unmistakable decadence of a declining culture. As a result of my Germanic studies, I attempted to elucidate these thousands of phenomena from a Christian point of view in a (quite inadequate) dissertation entitled *The History of the Eschatological Problem in German Literature*. From this evolved *Apocalypse of the German Soul*, my first book as a Jesuit, in which I tried to listen to the heartbeat of the great German poets and philosophers, ranging from Lessing, Herder, Kant, Goethe and Schiller to the German Idealists, and on to the central figure of Nietzsche, flanked by Kierkegaard and Dostoyevski, and across the Existentialist philosophers to Scheler, Karl Barth and Bloch. Hence the word *apocalypse*.

In the meantime I had entered the Society of Jesus. My philosophy professor was Erich Przywara, an excellent and unrelenting mentor. He forced one patiently to read scholastic philosophy and to engage at the same time (as he did) in modern thought. We had to confront Augustine and Aquinas with Hegel, Scheler and Heidegger. Later on, when I did my theology in Lyons, I encountered another dualism: no mention was ever made during lectures of a *nouvelle théologie* (I am wondering to this day how such a myth could have been invented for poor Fourvière!), but fortunately Henri de Lubac was in residence, and he referred us beyond scholasticism to the Church Fathers, generously making his notes and excerpts available to us. So it came about that while the others were playing soccer, I studied with Daniélou, Bouillard and a number of others (Fessard was no longer there), and I wrote books about Origen, Gregory of Nyssa and Maximus. During vacations I went to Munich in order to append a chapter to my German work. At one time it was Jean Paul, at another Hegel. During my years in Lyons I discovered the great French poets Claudel, Péguy and Bernanos—they have been my indispensable companions ever since. I translated Claudel's *Satin Slipper* at least five times before it reached its final version. (The first performance was in Zurich, in German, before the Parisian première.) On the Christian element in Bernanos I wrote a hefty volume, and I translated whatever was translatable of Péguy. Alas, *Eve* and *Tapisseries* were not in that category, but Corneille's *Polyeucte*, which Péguy considered the most important work in French literature, describes in detail the encounter of Christianity and culture as envisaged by him and also by me.

Finally, after my ordination, the Provincial gave me two choices: a teaching post at the Gregorian University or pastoral work with students. I chose the latter, and arrived in Basel at the beginning of 1940, where I met Karl Barth and Adrienne von Speyr (and Jaspers only at rare visits), but I will

12

while he talked of China and his work. I remember a marvelous encounter with Claudel in the city: he sat in the middle of a circle of admirers and veritably radiated goodness and wisdom. To every silly question he had a brilliantly clever, constructive answer. It was Henri de Lubac, however, who then taught at the Institut Catholique—unfortunately not at ours—who was the great stimulator. His *Catholicisme*, which had been in preparation for years, was actually the first authentic breakthrough into a more liberated view of the Church. I remember with horror a birthday celebration in honor of Fr. Yves Congar at which the master of ceremonies said something like this: no matter how important your work may be, that of de Lubac, not yours, has achieved the decisive breakthrough. De Lubac's book was a tapestry, a composition formed of selections from unknown Church Fathers and from the great theology of the saints—actually the oldest theology, which could only appear as *nouvelle théologie* to certain reactionaries. And as for his *Surnaturel*, for which he had to languish in the *Caves du Vatican* for decades, it was nothing else but the simple recovery of an important aspect of Augustine and Aquinas. At that time this constituted a heretical innovation for the most celebrated theology professors and to this day for certain cardinals, although these so-called innovations have become common currency for everyone. These have been misused by a few in an entirely

14

different form, in no way intended by the author. But now that we have taken up the subject, I should like to refer to two other aspects of his work, which have come into prominence in an unexpected way. First, his profound analysis and critique of Buddhism, particularly of Amida Buddhism, which seems to exhibit certain similarities with Christian grace and prayer; he brilliantly points out its dissimilarity to the Christian discipleship, whereas today a great number of Christians are following Zen without being aware of even the most elementary differences. And secondly, his relentless unmasking of Comte's atheistic Positivism, as outlined in *Le Drame de l'Humanisme athée*, while today Western culture is sliding into this very atheistic Positivism (under the name of *sciences humaines*), just as the East has fallen prey to its Marxist counterpart, so-called humanist Positivism.

Angelo Scola: During your student years at Fourvière, the Church was a well-ordered society. I am thinking of the discipline in the parishes and the great religious orders and also the tight organization of Catholic Action. These various structures aided the Church's mission in the world.

Hans Urs von Balthasar: Indeed they did. There were enough structures, probably too many, if measured by the inner vitality that should have animated them. I lack the experience to judge how much vitality actually existed in the parishes and seminaries at that time. And the religious orders: at Fourvière, there were some remarkable older Jesuits, and I have known many such in France and in other countries. But I was amazed with what speed, as I was to learn after my departure from Lyons, the inner structure, especially among the scholastics, dissolved and with what carelessness the best traditions of the Order were increasingly abandoned, so that the late Cardinal Daniélou, meanwhile labeled a reactionary, discouraged young people from entering the Order. In other religious communities, the interior collapse was at least equally visible, and it would be unjust to blame it on the after-effects of the Council.

Within all of them, numerous pathological symptoms erupted, long-latent in the organism. However, at this point I do not wish to generalize without drawing distinctions and denounce, for instance, the entire structure of Catholic Action as a shallow mechanism. It was certainly not that, at least not in France. But living organisms can harden and ossify to such a degree that it may not be advisable later to infuse them with new life. To put it in general terms: the fault is usually not with the structures as such but with the lack of authentic spirit that should animate them. Structure and organism are two different things. And mere structure without interior life is already worldliness. When the Council proclaimed the "opening

look, so that humanity can see the true Christ through me? The answer does not lie in the transformation of ecclesiastical structures, an all too common concern, but rather in what manner the Church can existentially become one single testimony to Christ, something which from her foundation and due to her objective constitution she already is. Nobody will convert to Christ because of a magisterium, sacraments, a clergy, canon law, apostolic nunciatures or a gigantic ecclesiastical machinery. Conversion will occur when a person encounters a Catholic who communicates the Christian message by his life and thus testifies that there exists not *a* but *the* believable imitation of Christ within the Catholic sphere. As a result, such a person, seeking Christ, will tolerate all the imperfections of the Church. The Council has expressed this lucidly in two documents: in *Lumen Gentium*, by the assertion that all Christians, not just a number of elect, are called to perfect love and holiness. (I may add parenthetically, that this has always been the program of the Ignatian Exercises: "that we ought to prepare ourselves to arrive at perfection of Christian love in whatever state or way of life God may grant us to choose.") A second conciliar document, *Dei Verbum*, goes even further by referring to the indivisibility of three elements: Holy Scripture, Tradition and Church Magisterium. Each of the three elements, for the sake of its identity, refers to the other two. No

Scripture without Tradition and Magisterium, no Tradition without Scripture and Magisterium, no Magisterium without Scripture and Tradition. This has always been known, but never before has it been expressed so concisely. There is not sufficient time here to follow through in every detail. One would have to demonstrate that only under these conditions can the entire people of God attain holiness and thus become a believable witness to Jesus Christ.

Angelo Scola: You mentioned two points in *Lumen Gentium*. Which is the other?

Hans Urs von Balthasar: This is a delicate subject, but one that cannot be evaded. *Lumen Gentium* has thoroughly examined the papacy and the episcopacy and in order to express their inherent relationship it coined an expression, *Communio Hierarchica*, which inextricably fuses two aspects. Let us first consider *Communio* in the sense of Saint Cyprian, who perceived the visible unity of the Church above all in the loving concord of all Catholic bishops in the world. That was his first insight, which he later supplemented with the loving concord of all bishops with the Bishop of Rome. Already his first concept is rich and profound and deserves to be treated by itself. The execution of the scheme does, however, presuppose one condition, the supranationalism of the Church, and this has but one adversary: nationalism, which erects barriers in the world as well as in the Church, dividing nations, cultures and races. Do you really believe that this adversary has been overcome in the Church? Or is it perhaps hiding behind the effort of certain bishops, perhaps under the slogan of "inculturation", to install national churches and corresponding national bishops' conferences, which should be invested with as much autonomy as possible, under the pretext that only then could the Church in a specific country or continent unfold organically and implement the program of *Lumen Gentium*? Were we not told that the true *Communio* within a country or continent was embodied by the bishops' conference, of which each bishop is a "member"? Viewed from such a perspective, one cannot help but conclude that the Universal Church consists of the sum total of national churches, and hence is not supranational but international.

I have no reason to suspect that such national structures confront each other in an antagonistic manner, as do the "blocs" in the international sphere. We have not arrived at that yet. Nevertheless, in today's Church it has become a political factor that the Pope is a Pole, and therefore is considered a foreigner within the national culture of Italy. It would be even more scandalous if a German were to intrude into the closed cultural milieu of France and remind them of certain basic articles that belong in every Catholic catechism. Latin American bishops and cardinals are traveling across Germany addressing Socialist networks about their liberation theology, without finding it necessary to inform the local ordinaries or calling on them. More examples could be cited, although they in no way constitute the rule. No, despite the lurking enemy, there exists a never-failing episcopal *Communio* in Cyprian's sense, reaching across national and continental boundaries. Its existence would, however, be gravely imperiled if one applied the word *Communio* to bishops' conferences, particularly in the case of the United States.

Now let us consider the second aspect, *Hierarchica*. What is meant here is the assemblage of the bishops under the unifying principle, which is represented by the Bishop of Rome. At this point one might enlarge upon the "anti-Roman complex", which, across the continents, is more rampant than ever, manifesting itself in the most diverse forms, which in the end are but variations on the same theme.

Angelo Scola: For instance?

Hans Urs von Balthasar: I do not wish to particularize now, perhaps we can refer to the subject later on, for it is the *articulus stantis vel cadentis ecclesiae*. You wish to hear examples? Well, first there is the already mentioned nationalism in the

Church, which seems to be on the increase and should not be confused with the conciliar term "local churches". Secondly, the distortion of the Council's concept "people" into "democracy", which would result in the loss of ecclesiastical obedience, which has christological roots. If the *Communio Hierarchica* of the bishops, and again of every single Christian, is not perceived and lived as a manifest imitation of Christ, all is in vain. As a result, any pastoral guidance in the Catholic sense becomes impossible, for its end is no longer the "body" and "bride" of Christ but a church-people, which feels and acts in a democratic fashion.

Angelo Scola: Let us not dwell on the Second Vatican Council any longer, on which your friend Cardinal de Lubac has spoken at great length. I would prefer to reflect with you on what is commonly called the postconciliar period. An introductory question: What influence have the conciliar documents exercised on your theological work?

Hans Urs von Balthasar: You know that I did not attend the Council and therefore did not share in experiencing the enthusiasm of its participants. The Council has produced a great number of papers, more perhaps than the average Catholic (or bishop) can master. And the abundance of the letter does, of course, by no means guarantee the abundance of the spirit. One can tell this by looking at the great documents, enduring in their strength, whereas the enormous amount of commentaries —justly or unjustly—are merely thumbed through by specialists. It is the spirit that counts; "the flesh", says Jesus, is "of no avail". I tried to listen carefully to that spirit, which rushes through the great forest of papers, although you will not detect many literal quotations in my work. This spirit, occasionally clad in somewhat antiquated forms, seems to me still so timely that it is useless to look forward to a Third Vatican Council. This spirit, I might add, would shine forth with even greater clarity if the texts were somewhat condensed and differently organized.

Angelo Scola: What relationship do you perceive between the Council and the crisis immediately following it?

Hans Urs von Balthasar: It has been observed before that a good deal of the preconciliar structures had become ossified. Moreover, the intention of *aggiornamento* (*mettre à jour*) has, of course, been thoroughly misunderstood. The Church was to be restored from within, from its most original sources, so that she may confront the modern world. This was taken as an occasion for secularizing the Church. The Pope and Cardinal Ratzinger are completely correct on this point: the postconciliar difficulties could not be blamed on the Council.

Angelo Scola: At the very root of the crisis lies a conflict of how to interpret the Council. It depends, I think, a great deal on another conflict of interpretation still of current interest in the Church, namely, what is to be understood by modernity. Are there, in your view, questions the modern world has addressed to the Church and which the Church has not known how to answer?

Hans Urs von Balthasar: There is no doubt that an anthropology will have to be constructed, in which all the dimensions discovered by the modern world can unfold and develop. In this undertaking one will frequently encounter specialized sciences with their own formulations, which will have to be taken seriously, although the Church cannot be expected to give authoritative answers while particular issues are still debated among specialists. What is needed, then, is an anthropology which is both up-to-date and Christian, that is to say, illuminated by the light of revelation. There exist elements in the natural sphere—it was Guardini who taught me to realize this—which reveal their significance only when touched by supernatural light. Such elements exist today, and here I should like to quote my cousin Peter Henrici, S.J., of the Gregorian University. He has pointed out in an important paper that we can no longer regard metaphysics the way the Greeks did. For them, *physis* was simply the cosmically all-embracing, whereas we are apt to regard man as the apex and epitome of the cosmos. Hence we ought to be transposing "meta-physics" into a "meta-anthropology", without, however, neglecting the meaning of "meta" in any way. Traces of this transposition of the Greek consciousness into the personal-Christian one are certainly present in Augustine and (according to the interpretation of J. B. Metz) in Saint Thomas as well. Still, a mere continuation of high- and late-Scholasticism will not be sufficient for this, although it may provide us with some valuable building stones. Once, however, the Christian is aware of the uniqueness of revelation, he may rely, while developing the human sciences, on spiritual discernment, which will guide his judgment in regard to the complexity of newly-evolving issues. This process may well require a period of sufficient reflection.

Angelo Scola: There exists, then, no distrust of modern culture, a culture the Church may not be able to embrace?

Hans Urs von Balthasar: Fundamentally not, if adequate spiritual discernment is exercised. It may point to some dangerous, even demonic, features of "modernity", features that make one wonder whether they are culturally constructive or rather the reverse.

Angelo Scola: Can you name some special instances?

Hans Urs von Balthasar: Yes, indeed, the mass media. It is well-known what a seductive influence they exert on young people, who, assaulted by a multitude of chaotic images flitting across the screen, are no longer capable of asking questions about the meaning of life. I remember one of the last lectures of Gabriel Marcel, at which, leaving his notes aside and glancing up at the ceiling, he said that watching television reminded him of seeing a tiny patch of the ocean floor through the hatch of a submarine, imagining it to be the whole world. And yet I can recognize something even more unsettling for a Christian, something for which I could cite many examples. In rectories, the pastor spends every night in front of the television, no matter whether he has said his Office or not. He scarcely reads anything. The same applies to monasteries. I know of religious houses where the scholastics watch television until midnight instead of doing their studies. And if one looks at the viewing-habits in Carmelite convents, one begins to wonder why there exists a cloister at all! It is incalculable how much prayer is lost for the Church and the world due to the media, how many treasures God has been robbed of, and of

"objectless" contemplation of the living God, who is triune love and who revealed himself in the humanity of Jesus Christ and his Holy Spirit, in which case, in a Christian sense, no abstraction is possible. It would result in a de-incarnation. The second danger consists in the attempt to experience God directly (charismatically) by some psychological-religious technique of heightened self-awareness, no matter whether initiated by "group dynamics" or by any other technique. A recent book on the subject bears the characteristic title: *Gotteserfahrung im Schnellverfahren* (Experiencing God in Fast Motion). What is essential, however, is not a confidently mastered technique but surrender of the self to that which God in his love bestows on those who firmly believe in him. A third danger is different still: it is well known that contemplative abbeys, especially in France, are overcrowded, whereas the few seminaries still in existence remain virtually empty. Young people are in search of a life dedicated to God, and what is offered in preparation for the priesthood does not convince them. Profound absorption in God's mysteries, which is the necessary introduction to their priestly activities, is not guaranteed, and for this reason they flee into monasteries. I suspect that many find refuge there who normally would have chosen pastoral work. All this says little about the essence of Christian contemplation, but perhaps the area within which it should be situated is negatively defined.

by today's biblical exegesis, which is itself largely a child of the Enlightenment. It raises questions which ordinary Christians, with their naïve understanding of the Bible, can no longer master. It raises a problem for theologians as well: by what method is a strictly scientific exegesis of Scripture compatible with a spiritual understanding of it, as the Fathers and the Middle Ages knew it? That both can go seriously hand in hand has been clearly demonstrated by such people as, above all, Heinrich Schlier, a pupil of Bultmann and a convert to Catholicism, also Heinz Schürmann, Stanislas Lyonnet, Ignace de la Potterie, Jerome Quinn, to name but a few. What is required is an ability to answer questions prompted by the Enlightenment in regard to Christ and Christianity with greater substance and depth than some specialized exegetes are in the habit of doing. Across the range of problems arising from textual criticism, it is possible to confront the primal phenomenon of Christ, which could never have retained the unique and indestructible authority it radiated throughout the centuries by a process of subsequent "overpainting". Primal phenomena are not created by patchwork, a fact recognized by modern Homeric research, and Homer is by no means Christ. Exegesis has provided us with much that is valuable and taught us to see things in their gradual development. What it cannot do is convince us that the Bible is nothing but a literary document amongst many; for within the framework of world literature it remains unique in its incomparable witness to the self-manifestation of God. Those whom Christ called "the simple" comprehend directly "what is hidden from the worldly-wise". The ultimate answer the Church has to offer to the Enlightenment is, beyond all reasoning, the simple witness which the apostles and saints have borne in the past, and which the persecuted Church is bearing now. She thus exists in direct imitation of her Lord, who, being the Word of God, did nothing but bear witness to him who uttered it, and because of this, was persecuted and crucified.

Angelo Scola: I remember a lecture you gave fifteen years ago at Einsiedeln, in which you developed the relationship between modern culture and the Jews.

Hans Urs von Balthasar: This leads us into one of the most complex questions, one perhaps God alone can answer correctly. We are dealing here with that original Schism within the one people of God (for there cannot be two), which Christ himself has brought about with full responsibility, and therefore the Church should not act as if she knew the solution and could bring it about on her own. We are presented only with fragments of the whole truth, and we lack the capacity of making them into a whole. It is indeed alarming that the fate of the broken Covenant should have been sealed as early as five hundred years before Christ. This was the time when God stopped the prophets from praying for a people that had shown itself reprobate and was to be sent into exile. In some manner this colossal event, apparently definitive, served as a model for the even greater one, which culminated in the rejection of Jesus. The lengthy interim was still able to produce such beauties as the late Psalms. The pharisees, successors of the Maccabees, in their zeal, wished to prove to God that one can keep the law, but according to Saint Paul and to Jesus himself, they fell into the pit they had dug for themselves. Their house is "left desolate" (Mt 23:38), a fact which cannot be changed by the "State of Israel", itself for the most part atheistic. All Israel can do is wait for the ultimate prophecy which Jesus himself proclaimed ("until you shall say . . .") and which Peter (Acts 3:19) and Paul (Rom 11) have ratified. Karl Barth's theory of predestination, in which he pleads for a single people of God, consisting of both Jews and Christians, has always affected me profoundly. He compares the two peoples with the two who suffer on the left and right of the Crucified. One, turning away into darkness, the other, turning toward the light, with the hands of Christ stretched out in both directions.

Angelo Scola: I am interrupting here, because what you said touches upon an important point. If Israel continues to belong to the people of God even after the birth of the Church, what meaning then can "people of God", the name given to the Church by the Council, convey?

Hans Urs von Balthasar: Even if Israel continues to belong to the people of God, one must not overlook the distinction Saint Paul has explicitly drawn between a people according to the flesh and one according to the spirit. Let me recall the fundamentally opposite movements we mentioned initially. The mystery of Israel consists in being both an "ethnic" people with certain racial characteristics (no gentile can in that sense ever become a Jew) and also a people created and preserved by God with a special purpose. Both aspects, the ethnic and the theological one, are inseparable as long as a Jew confesses his Jewishness—or negatively expressed—does not become a Christian, that is, move from the theology of the Old Testament to that of the New, which is its fulfillment. This amalgamation was already a paradox during the Old Dispensation, and the Jews have remained aware of it to this day: Israel was an ethnic reality, enclosed in itself, destined, however, (Deutero-Isaiah) to become a light to all nations. Its election presented an event for the entire world as early as Abraham; one can observe this characteristic in Martin Buber or in any other outstanding Jewish figure of today: there always exists a consciousness that Israel constitutes a model people for humanity in general. That this consciousness could remain alive throughout the tragic history of the Jews is a proof for the ongoing theological relationship between the Israel of the Old Testament and that of today: "God does not repent of his promises." Nevertheless, after the mission of the Baptist "to turn the children of Israel to their Lord and God" had failed (Lk 1:16), his successor, Jesus, could no longer summon the "ethnic" Israel to his spiritual office; being the last and all-embracing Word of God, he himself was the origin of an "Israel of God" (as Saint Paul calls the Church), no longer bound by any ethnic ties. The "New Covenant in my blood"—and here the Jews are correct—is not new in the sense of suspending the Old Testament; it rather perfects it by dissolving what is bound by the flesh (circumcision) in favor of a new eucharistic corporeality, based on and founded by Christ (baptism). Considering this elevation of the particular to the universal or catholic, I venture a hypothesis of my own, which I am not forcing on anyone: that a Jew who becomes a Christian ceases therewith to be a Jew, just as a gentile who becomes Christian ceases to be a gentile. Salvation assuredly comes "*out* of the Jews", as Jesus says in the Gospel of Saint John, but Saint Paul, the Christian, in order to convert his brothers, behaves not *as* a Jew, but "*like* a Jew" "to them who are under the law, as one under the law, although myself *not* under the law" (1 Cor 9:20). For the Jew who converts to Christ, the Old Testament paradox, that a people can have theo-

34

logical significance in a universal sense, has been transcended.

This by no means implies that a Jew who enters the Church does not remain deeply and existentially tied to the people of his origins, more deeply perhaps than any gentile can understand. "In the Holy Spirit", Saint Paul gives testimony of his "great sadness", of "the incessant grief in his heart", because his brothers in the flesh, on whom such infinite graces have been bestowed, even "Christ himself having descended from them in the flesh", were not able to follow his path. So powerfully does he experience the bond with Israel that were it possible he would forego his own salvation for their sake, "be cursed apart from Christ", if only they could find the salvation which he has attained. This text belongs to the most paradoxical of the entire Bible. It is an extreme manifestation of Christian, even christological, love, the desire to co-experience the "pro nobis" of Christ to the utmost; Christ who had been made "sinful" and "accursed" in our stead, not in an external, merely juridical sense, but by vicariously experiencing the curse of sin in the timeless inescapability of the Cross and the "descent into hell". At this point it becomes apparent what a step Saint Paul had taken, when he crossed over from the Old Testament to the New. "Accursed" did not for him mean something temporary, anymore than it did for the Savior on the Cross; Paul, the Christian, not only wished to share, from love and kinship, the theological destiny of his brothers in Israel, but desired to assume it in their stead.

You ask why the Church, beside Israel, can be described as people of God. My answer is this: in a metaphorical sense, as are, according to *Lumen Gentium*, metaphorical all the other designations of the Church, namely, images for a reality which is veiled in mystery. Besides, it should not be forgotten that such descriptive expressions as "people" are Old Testament quotations in their entirety. Cardinal Ratzinger has justly emphasized that "people" cannot be the central statement about the Church: "body" and "bride" of Christ reach a deeper understanding of the mystery.

Angelo Scola: I should like once more to return to the Jews, in order to discuss their connection with the important atheistic movements of the present, primarily with Marxism. It seems to me that you mentioned this at Einsiedeln.

Hans Urs von Balthasar: I do not recall it. However, according to a number of serious scholars both Jewish and non-Jewish, it is undeniable that Marxism presents a fundamentally secularized messianic phenomenon. Theunissen has collected such evidence in his book on Hegel. In reading Martin Buber's hasidic novel *Gog und Magog* with regard to the historic actuality of Israel, one realizes that for him, who believed in a universal Jewish mission, the choice was between two possibilities: either wait for the Messiah, or, since he fails to appear, carry out his mission. Two modes, then, of understanding the Deutero-Isaian prophecy. The second mode has been adopted by atheistic Jewry. To that extent Marxism constitutes a negative-theological phenomenon. And to that extent Israel remains an explosive center in the international arena.

Angelo Scola: There exists an intellectual current which proceeds from historicity as the basic theological reality. It holds that the Council did not consider man in his historical situation. And objectively speaking one must admit that only certain passages in *Gaudium et Spes* meet this demand. What is your view on this?

Hans Urs von Balthasar: I am not sure whether the theology you are speaking of has sufficiently grasped the essence of the revelation which the Church proclaims. If the Christian revelation is truly eschatological and if we are not to expect—as do the countless Joachimites—a qualitatively new age of the Spirit, then I cannot imagine a historical "situation" of man and mankind for which the Church's witness to God, who so much loved the world that he surrendered his beloved, would have become obsolete. One must not forget that the Church, although she makes her way alongside world history, is at her center *supra*historical, anchored in the definitive and eternal. The letter to the Hebrews uses precisely this image of the anchor, dropped in eternity. The Church may vary her means of communication when faced with various historical situations, but the substance of what is revealed surpasses these differences, because it is timelessly valid. Thus the vocabulary, the disposition of the catechisms and the method of preaching may change; the substance, however, remains the same.

Angelo Scola: Among the writings you have produced during the seventies, there are two which are extremely critical of the Christian tendency toward a "secular world" (*Who Is a Christian?*) and an "anonymous Christianity" (*Cordula*). Were not the positions you attacked in earnest about the historical situation of man?

Hans Urs von Balthasar: To begin with the latter: I openly admit that I have never understood what place Rahner's categorical and transcendental categories, which he borrowed from Kant, can occupy in a Christian theology. Apparently Erich Przywara could not understand it either, for—according to Msgr. Strobl—he asked Rahner at a meeting in Vienna: "What on earth are they for?" That Rahner wished to open the door to salvation for the countless persons lacking explicit faith in Christ is certain; his theological inquiries were predominantly motivated by pastoral concern. But were the old notions of *Fides Implicita*, *Baptismus in Voto* and so forth not sufficient? I see a contradiction in the slogan "anonymous Christian", for a Christian is by definition one who receives his name from bearing witness to Christ. This slogan, by necessity, became the starting point for a trivialization of what it means to be a Christian, although Rahner had not intended it. One need only to take a look at certain American theologians who openly refer to Rahner, to realize what a feeble affair being a Christian can become: through Christ the news has come into the world that God is above all a God of love and not of vengeance; that grace is at work even in those who have not expressly invoked it, as long as they sincerely (a favorite expression with Rahner) follow their consciences; that, according to McBrien, one need not talk about Original Sin any longer; and, above all, that Jesus did not carry the Cross in substitution for sinful man. In the end, out of aversion for the satisfaction theory of Saint Anselm, Rahner openly taught that the Church can forego the *pro nobis* of the Cross; that only a (so-called "late") theology of Saint Paul had introduced it; that nobody can really carry the sins of another, and thus the Cross represented simply the sign of God's full "solidarity" with us sinners. A very strange sign, I

On Liberation Theology

Angelo Scola: Yes, in the second instance we are dealing with the "tendency toward a secular world". Are we not now approaching the problem of liberation theology?

Hans Urs von Balthasar: I think we are. Liberation theology is primarily a political re-reading of Old and New Testament texts. It leans heavily on the prophetic messages of the Old Testament, which deal with the wrath of Yahweh over the oppression of the poor in Israel. And since Israel is in the before-mentioned sense an "ethnic" people, this theology may indeed be called biblical, not however, truly and properly Christian. It is biblical because, as we have already said, Israel represents a unique blend of ethnic and theological components. Nevertheless, as early as the Old Covenant, the concept of "the poor" begins to shift from a more sociological to a theological one. Since Jeremiah, the "poor of Yahweh" are those who can put their trust in no temporal power but in God alone. That the predominantly theological factor of Yahweh's poor does not exclude but rather includes the political one, has been lucidly demonstrated by the late Pierre Ganne, a dear friend of mine, whose small book *Le Pauvre et le Prophete* (the prophetic role of the poor) I translated. He shows in it that the poor are not only theologically but also politically the true prophets, for they stake their all, beyond earthly millennialisms, on the absolute future of God.

But what happens when we pass from the Old Testament to the New? Have we not already made this transition when we distinguish between a temporal "future" and an eternal "*avenir*" (which already has begun presently in Jesus Christ and his Holy Spirit)? We have now arrived at an essential factor, which Käsemann called eschatological anticipation, a central characteristic of the New Testament. And now I have to ask the question I am always impelled to ask when I read the texts of liberation theology: is not everything already contained in the dual commandment of Jesus, in his truly eschatological maxim, "What you have done to the least of my brethren . . ."? Is the much-invoked solidarity with the poor not clearly manifest in this commandment? Is it necessary to invent an additional theology for desperate sociological situations, a theology which runs the risk of constructing something alongside what has always been understood by serious Christians and which could result in being less comprehensive, less Christian than the Gospels? It is, of course, true that entire epochs have averted their eyes from its ethical and political demands, soothing their consciences with a morality of alms-giving. In this respect it is all for the good that we are now inexorably confronted by the old biblical radicalism, as preached by Saint John Chrysostom and lived by Saint Francis and Saint Peter Claver. But does this really require a new Christology as presented by Leonardo Boff, just to mention one of its outstanding proponents?

Angelo Scola: What is new in this Christology?

Hans Urs von Balthasar: One can recognize it clearly in his book *Paixão de Christo, paixão do mundo* (Petropolis, 1978). In it, Boff seems to develop a Christology strongly influenced by Bultmann, with whom he suggests that we know very little about the historical Jesus. However, he believes that we can interpret the primary intention of Jesus as that of someone who understood himself in his role as liberator of the poor and oppressed. Everything else in the story of Jesus he leaves aside as irrelevant, even confusing and harmful over-painting, notwithstanding the fact that the Gospel versions and their interpretation by Saint Paul, as well as that of the entire Tradition, have been determined by it. The liberation—the "Kingdom of God", which Jesus expected to result from it—had failed to come about, as expressed by the authentic cry on the Cross: "Why hast thou forsaken me?" The doctrine of substitution is rejected by Boff as well as by Rahner. It is up to us present-day Christians to adopt and execute what Jesus had wished and begun.

And since we are speaking of Boff's christological design, a word might be added about his Mariology, which contains much that is beautiful and in agreement with Tradition, though its main theme throws a curious light on his Christology. The fundamental thesis (delivered as hypothesis, but finished in detail), which apparently intends to capture the feminist movement by investing it with theological depth, is emphasized in italic print: Mary, who is the eschatologically highest realization of the feminine, was overshadowed by the Holy Spirit in such a way that she can and must be described as hypostatically united with the Spirit. This thesis rests on two bases: one, the theory of C. G. Jung which posits that in every person, man or woman, a masculine (*animus*) and a feminine (*anima*) element are present. Thus the two sexes are created to complement each other, and in their union each finds the other as well as its own self. Starting from here, Boff proceeds to say of the hypostatic union of Jesus Christ, that in him not only the masculine but also the feminine are essentially united to the Divine Logos. Nevertheless, it is precisely because of this union that a complementary one is to be expected: a corresponding union, predominantly feminine, must be accomplished, if only because the suprasexual God is the

44

authors who are both close to his basic intention, but develop it in an orthodox form: Teilhard de Chardin, with his vision of the *Eternel Féminin* (commented by Cardinal de Lubac), and Louis Bouyer's bold thesis, influenced by Russian Sophiology, in which he holds that the entire world process rests upon the union of the (descending) Logos with Sophia (ascending to Mary). With both authors, the virginal motherhood of Mary presents the last and highest flowering of Sophia striving upward within the world process, just as Christ presents the definitive Incarnation of the Logos, increasingly made concrete by the same process. Both, accordingly, do not form two hypostatic unions, which as such would have to depict the suprasexual masculine-femininity of God, but precisely that nuptial "toward each other", which Saint Paul (Eph 5) and the entire tradition describe in countless Christian commentaries on the Canticle of Canticles. Then, of course, keeping in mind the whole of tradition, the equal dignity of man and woman must be corroborated by their division of roles as delineated by Saint Paul (1 Cor 11), and finally converge again in equal dignity, when he concludes: "In the Lord woman is neither dependent on man, nor is man dependent on woman, for just as woman stems from man, so man is from woman. All, however, stem from God." I do not believe that this can be fundamentally surpassed. But enough of liberation theology, although it possesses many other variants than the one we have described here.

Angelo Scola: Is not liberation an integral part of the missionary mandate of Christ, and is it not necessary for any genuine inculturation?

Hans Urs von Balthasar: Indeed, it is. However, to recapitulate, it does not presuppose any new theology, but rather an effective Christian witness to the main commandment. Consider the work of Mother Teresa of Calcutta. Not her theology, but her Christian actions have astounded the Indian sages and brought her to the attention of the entire world. And, strangely enough, she did not even have to touch upon the complex problems of inculturation. It is well known that these problems increase in difficulty when Christianity is brought face to face with more elaborate and sophisticated cultures, as is the case in India, where philosophical wisdom and perspicacity surpass Christian philosophizing. Not that missionary work is any easier in the case of certain African tribes, whose spiritual traditions need also to be respected, or in the case of Latin American Indians, Eskimos or Papuas. Perhaps the example of Mother Teresa teaches us that the living model presents the best access to the Gospel message. On the other hand, the unique

47

phenomenon of Christ is not wedded to any "culture", even to the hellenistic one of the Mediterranean. Saint Paul knew this. So did the German and Slavic missionaries, as well as Augustine of Canterbury, when he was sent to England by Pope Gregory. Of course, Jesus remains the fulfiller of the Old Covenant for every culture. If one wishes to have Jesus without the Old Testament, or replace his antecedents by one's own culture (African or Asiatic), the result will resemble Hitler's "German Christians".

Is There a Christian Culture?

Angelo Scola: Why do Western Christians appear to perceive the alliance of faith and culture as problematical? Is there indeed a sense in which we can speak of Christian culture?

Hans Urs von Balthasar: There certainly should be. Unfortunately we are now immersed in a culture which should rather be called a technical civilization in its final stage, in which we run the risk of being overwhelmed and dehumanized by a man-made machine, from which we promised ourselves freedom, only to be robbed of it. By machine is meant not only the "frame", as Heidegger named it, but the entire pseudo-human bureaucratic machinery, as denounced earlier by Marx. How should one go about freeing man from a prison he has built for himself and create an authentic Christian culture? How can we free him from a contrivance of world-wide dimensions, which is almost automatically self-perfecting? Politics and economics are so inextricably entangled that no one apparently is able to bring this wheel-work to a standstill. One cannot help wondering whether the liberation theologians sufficiently accounted for the global proportions of this phenomenon. In the foreground one can certainly divide people into the "oppressors" and the "oppressed". But is it taken into consideration that the oppressors in the foreground are or may be themselves the oppressed in the background and that it will be difficult indeed from here on to find the Ultimate Oppressor? Perhaps they all belong to the oppressing oppressed —which in no way should imply that everyone is an innocent lamb.

Angelo Scola: And if you were asked to give a brief definition of Christian culture?

Hans Urs von Balthasar: I do not know if it is possible to deal with it in a brief fashion. Culture is a loosely-knit word. Originally it meant the cultivation of the soil, as mentioned in Genesis: to make nature's wilderness humanly habitable, to put the imprint of man upon it. During certain cultural epochs this enterprise may have succeeded to a degree; let us remember the *Georgics* by Virgil. But what can be done amid this want of culture wrought by the machine? I suppose one can try to build islands of humanity, and in this project Christians could and should be leading; such actions may have a contagious effect on others and stimulate an asceticism which renounces the excessive goods of consumerism, simply to become more human. In the Eastern bloc countries, where life is almost exclusively dictated by bureaucracy, such islands of freedom are immediately recognized and sought. "When everything is blocked off," I was told by a dear friend who lives in Erfurt, "one must try to live in the interstices." Apparently the Christians of the Apocalypse, though they did not bear the sign of the beast, had discovered or created such spaces. From islands like this, true culture, Christian culture, may spread across the earth. Many people are athirst for it.

Angelo Scola: When addressing Catholics, John Paul II has repeatedly called for a transition from faith to culture, emphasizing that faith must create culture, from which specific ways of living can evolve.

Hans Urs von Balthasar: That should indeed be possible, remembering God's original commandment, for God cannot have commanded the impossible. If man was appointed ruler of the animal kingdom and nature, he must possess this ability within himself, even when, as a result of its misuse, his products have reduced him to a state of servitude. All this sounds very abstract, but the Gospel does not give concrete instructions concerning Christian culture. Nevertheless, such instructions are implicit in Christ's mandate to give testimony, if necessary, by blood (Apocalypse). Such testimony is given by the epistles of Saint Paul, by the marvelous letter to Philemon, every word of which presents Christian humanism. Testimony, too, consists in doing "whatever things are true, honorable, just, holy, lovable, worthy of praise" (Phil 4:8). To be consistently Christian means to be consistently human, if only because no other religion demands and shows such reverence for one's neighbor as well as the body as does the religion of the incarnate, of Christ and his dual commandment.

Angelo Scola: Within the dramatic scope of our society, which you have sketched, to what should a Christian commit himself?

Hans Urs von Balthasar: A Christian should commit himself to the whole of secular culture. Today this is chiefly realized by the secular institutes, one of which I have started to develop with Adrienne von Speyr. The idea is to commit oneself on all levels on which a Christian commitment can humanize whatever is threatening to slide into the inhuman.

Angelo Scola: What should a Christian do, what stance should he take in the arena of politics? Some believe that one ought to "exhibit an ethical-professional profile". Is that sufficient?

Hans Urs von Balthasar: We cannot simply entrust politics to non-Christians. The Church is confronted with political systems in the world—and by no means merely peripherally. They are to be taken seriously, even though they may present a heavy burden for the Christian. This presupposes, of course, professional competence, just as a physician or lawyer must exhibit competence in his field. This idea is basic to all secular institutes. What applies to secular professions applies equally to politics: although we cannot force specifically Christian ethics on non-Christians, we nevertheless have to demonstrate that life according to such terms is humanly believable. It is faith as exemplified in one's life that makes the specialist credible, even when there is no need to preach it. Take, for example, *Markings* by Dag Hammarskjöld.

A sufficient treatment of the thorny theme "Mission and conduct of a Christian politician", however, exceeds the scope of this interview and, above all, my competence. How can consideration for the common good of the secular state, only to a small degree consciously Christian, and consideration for the individual conscience and knowledge of the politician be harmonized? Are there any objectively verifiable norms, or must the Christian conscience of the politician freely decide each case for itself? In the end he alone can decide whether his missionary obligation as a Christian may have to be reserved in a particular instance, due to a more urgent or seemingly opportune consideration, which may permit him to serve more effectively in the long run.

Angelo Scola: Finally, then, the central issue is the missionary task of every Christian, which cannot be evaded. But how is the essence of Christianity to be communicated to contemporary men and women?

Hans Urs von Balthasar: Primarily, by confronting them uncompromisingly with the whole Gospel. With the whole Christ, rather than with a charism chosen at random. There is but one answer to the fundamental questions of humanity, and that is the Christian one. We are constantly returning to the same starting point: people need to recognize the incomparable, the unique character of the Gospel, not comparable to anything else in the rest of the world. In the universal history of humanity there does not exist—and never will exist—anything analogous to Christ, a man who, without presumption, speaks and acts with the authority of God. "You have heard it said . . . I, however, am telling you." This "I" has the weight of the voice of Yahweh. And it is not only a matter of speaking. The entire existence of Jesus, his working life, his preaching, his death and Resurrection; everything in him is an exegesis of God. If one attempts to carve out a "historical Jesus" apart from his totality, one loses all understanding, just as the disciples understood nothing when confronted with his Passion and Transfiguration.

Angelo Scola: You equate, then, Christ the man with the Word of God?

Hans Urs von Balthasar: There exists no Christ figure in the New Testament which could be isolated from the sacraments, from the magisterial or pastoral Office or from Tradition. There is a great danger nowadays: to dissect Christ into several small parts, single *logoi* as it were, and then to meditate on this or that singular aspect, only to lose the vision of the whole. There are certain theologians who close their eyes to the overwhelming apostolic authority of Saint Paul, claiming that he possessed no such authority in the Christian communities; and such folly commands a wide audience. They also claim that in his day there was no hierarchy, no episcopacy, as if that had been necessary, as long as Saint Paul himself was bishop of his communities, together with Titus, Timothy and others, whom one would call auxiliary bishops today. When he sends one of them to Corinth, he impresses on the congregation: "Receive him the way you receive me, with the same reverence." Saint Paul was highly aware of his authority. And for his part, he acknowledges the authority of Saint Peter.

Angelo Scola: In speaking of Christ, you have used two words which struck me: "unique phenomenon". How can we deal with this uniqueness nowadays? After all, this is no private event, for which it would be sufficient to read the Bible by oneself or even with the aid of an experienced exegete.

Hans Urs von Balthasar: You are right. Holy Scripture is not preeminently "a" book, but a witness to the word of God, which was sent forth to us in Christ. This word has been written down, so that we may have something solid to support us. It is, however, not Christ's will that we read him like a book; he himself has written nothing: "My words are spirit and life." During the lifetime of the apostles and immediately afterward, there existed no "New Testament". The apostles proclaimed the life of Christ, and they did this with their own lives. Saint Paul is not presumptuous when he says: "Observe me, Christ lives in me; imitate Christ the way I imitate him." And further: "You have accepted the word for what it really is: not my word, but the word of Christ." The word of God cannot be simply recited, but requires the testimony of a living Christian, because the Word had become flesh; and hence one has to demonstrate with one's flesh what the word is.

Angelo Scola: But this living model should really be the Church?

Hans Urs von Balthasar: Of course. To the degree in which she realizes the fundamental intention of Jesus: to be a missionary Church.

The Anti-Roman Attitude

Angelo Scola: One of our mutual friends, Father Sicari, O.C.D., has recently sent me ten pages to be included in a book entitled *La Chiesa del Concilio Studi e Contributi*. The Institute ISTRA is in the process of publishing it. In this book, which also contains contributions by Cardinal Ratzinger, Sicari presents us with an original thesis. Using a work by Cardinal de Lubac, *La Posterité spirituelle de Joachim de Fiore*, he maintains that making the Church responsible for the present crisis is a Joachimian idea.

Hans Urs von Balthasar: This is extremely interesting. My own book, *The Office of Peter*, points in the same direction. This book should be written anew, because the anti-Roman attitude has greatly intensified among Catholics in recent years. Hardly a day goes by when the newspapers do not hurl vehement and vitriolic accusations at the Pope, at Cardinal Ratzinger, in fact at everything that originates from Rome. They were pounced on hysterically—for example, the gentleman who felt it to be his duty to stamp Ratzinger's interview [the *Ratzinger Report*] to the ground, three weeks before its German publication. There were passionate attacks from a handful of French bishops, fiercely angry ones from England—taking up an entire edition of "New Blackfriars"—and if one added the remarks of the clergy, mostly in Switzerland and in Germany, the list would become endless. Everywhere this anti-Roman mentality is at work, trying to press toward a point where the objective structures of the Church would be finally surpassed. This was the idea of the pious Abbot Joachim, and it is perhaps significant that he was of Jewish ancestry: he thought along futuristic-messianic lines. He, who was praised by several popes, hardly wished to destroy the Church. Our contemporaries, on the other hand, who give vent to their rage against Rome, work, intentionally or not, toward the destruction of the Church. (Concerning Joachim's Jewish ancestry, Cardinal de Lubac expressed himself with reserve in an earlier work, more definitely in a later. One could guess at this fact almost a priori when reading Joachim: for the first time someone—an Abbot!—seeks to overcome the institutional Church in the name of the Holy Spirit, in order to arrive at a purely spiritual Christianity freed from all official fetters. He did this in good faith, whereas our contemporaries, who, of course, call themselves Catholics, wish to undermine the Church which has reared them and saw off the branch on which they are sitting. They do this, thanks to an illusion of a free, democratic Church, in no way different from a liberal–Protestant Christianity.) The anti-Roman

character which she needs in the world. Neither can there be any doubt about the will of the Holy See to acquaint itself with the points of view and concerns of the various cultures and to give them room, as far as this is compatible with the unity of the Church. There exists no more attentive a listener than our Pope. The corresponding question, whether the immutable unity of the Body of Christ with the diversity of its members is correctly viewed by the representatives of the particular cultures and churches, cannot be so unequivocally answered.

There is, however, something to be said about the episcopal conferences, which, incidentally, vary considerably from each other, and about the desire of individual bishops for greater freedom of movement. Let us begin with the situation of the individual bishop. More than ever before, his freedom to make decisions has been curtailed from below as well as from above. The "decentralization" of the Roman Curia has led directly to the curialization of the diocese. In some countries, the diocesan machine has been inflated to an unprecedented degree, not to mention the pastoral councils, which since Vatican II have been added on all levels: that of the diocese, the deanery and the parish. Dioceses in Germany are administered by approximately a hundred to five hundred employees, and I would say, without having seen the statistics, that the total number of ecclesiastical positions in the country approaches several thousand, all of them on full salaries which in all likelihood exceed by many times those of the Vatican. The bishop is severely hampered in his movements, because he now is forced to avail himself of expert advice from all the proper organizations. Added to this are the permanent offices of the national conferences of bishops, which are supposed to free the individual bishop of much work. Alas, it is work proper to the individual bishop, responsibilities which have been withdrawn from him, a regrettable fact as far as the good of the Church is concerned. Perhaps these responsibilities were renounced voluntarily and in good faith, perhaps the bishops were overruled by common vote. Which brings me to the second infringement, the one from above, namely the episcopal conference. It is no secret that individual bishops, if one has the opportunity to speak with them privately, have views considerably different from the views expressed in the statements of the bishops' conference, at which they were either out-voted or did not dare venture an opinion. One wonders how many individual bishops have actually drafted and proposed one of these resounding pronouncements of the conference in the United States, which numbers about three hundred members. I suspect very few. These documents are sanctioned and signed by the bulk of the members (of which, I understand only two percent hold a doctorate in theology), who are often quite ignorant of the range and importance of the issues

in the Church which is impersonal or abstract, no matter whether these charisms are outstanding or simple and commonplace. Christ never instituted bureaus and committees; such institutions cannot make the central meditation on the choice (*elección*), as advocated in the Exercises of Saint Ignatius, in which each individual seeks to discover with what charism God wishes to endow him within the Body of Christ. For that reason Cardinal de Lubac, in his book on the unity of the Church, and after him Cardinal Ratzinger, indicated within what precise limits episcopal conferences and other such useful institutions may legitimately operate within the personal structure of the Church. The main point is this: every shepherd has his personal responsibility which he must not allow to be curtailed from below or from above. "Take heed to yourselves and to the whole flock in which the Holy Spirit has placed you as a bishop, to rule the Church of God, which he has purchased with his blood" (Acts 20:28). Nothing in the Church is impersonal and abstract, everything is concretely personal.

Angelo Scola: You have mentioned charisms. They are much talked about today. But what relationship do they have to Office?

Hans Urs von Balthasar: I have just tried to express the decisive factor from the standpoint of Saint Paul. Every permanent Office is a charism but not every charism is by any means a permanent Office. We have mentioned before that Saint Paul was deeply aware of his official authority; under no circumstances would he have placed it on the same level as his gift of healing or glossolalia (which, by the way, he maintained he possessed to a greater degree than others; he mentions the miracles he performed in Corinth only incidentally). Certainly Timothy should strongly guard his charism, which was imparted to him by the laying on of hands. An Office of the Church is not merely imparted externally, by episcopal decree, unless there simultaneously ensues a call from God. Karl Rahner has brilliantly elucidated this. The Office, which no doubt goes back to Christ, emerged in its fullest sense as early as the first century, when it functioned clearly in a contemporary sense. Clement of Rome, without doubt the city's bishop, (although the testimony of Irenaeus is questioned today without serious grounds), expressly demands obedience (*hypokoē*) from the obstinate Corinthians, and several years later the Roman Church is, according to the bishop and charismatic, Ignatius, "presiding in love" with every local church structured by the bishop and presbytery. And since Ignatius addresses all the communities he visits, no one can say that he was merely propagating an Antiochian hobby. The Holy Spirit, who builds up the Body of Christ, is both an objective and subjective spirit; Office and charism may exist in certain tension;

they are, however, not contradictions. I am again referring to Augustine, in whose life and work the unity of the two "undivided and unconfused" aspects of ecclesiastical existence are truly visible.

Angelo Scola: The tension between life and structure is central in today's debate. Some say that, due to an excessively structured center, life is pushed to the periphery.

Hans Urs von Balthasar: I recognize in these Catholic debates a curious blindness, considering that the present Pope demonstrates so convincingly—as did many popes of our century, but he in particular —the genuine vitality which must radiate from the Office. He lives on constant prayer, not on the promulgation of official texts. Even his encyclicals, which he composes himself—think of *Dives in Misericordia*—are but an example of Christian living. I must admit that in spite of my great admiration for Father Congar's magnificent *oeuvre*, I have always felt a bit uneasy when I came upon "life and structure" or "life and institution" opposing each other. I myself need to have an image before me: within the human organism the bones, too, are alive and indispensable; otherwise man could not stand straight and carry out an infinite variety of free movements. To repeat: the Church, living and official, is one single body, and any attempt to transfer this vitality to the particular churches, and to decry Rome as a mere structure, is destructive of *catholica*. Any form of nationalism or Gallicanism is a mortal blow. And if ossification has to be mentioned at all, its center is plainly not in Rome but at the so-called periphery: in the persistent obstinacy of the extreme progressivists as well as the extreme traditionalists. I can observe both these excesses diagnosed and energetically rejected by a thoughtful and critical youth, intent on helping to build a living Church.

as genuinely Catholic and open movements, but gradually shut themselves off, apparently in the belief of being sufficiently Catholic for themselves. One might call *Comunione e Liberazione* almost an exception: aside from a few missteps it is a good example of a movement which remains open. I am by no means saying that it is the only one, but it exemplifies how a Catholic movement must exist for the Church and for the world, not exclusively for itself. The traditionalist movements, on the contrary, only confirm this statement. More than ever before, there appears a danger that such movements view themselves as absolute: "Come and join us, we are the true Catholic Church!" If charisms are exclusively personal, they can hardly claim the Holy Spirit of the Church for themselves: it is from the wholeness of the Church that he distributes his gifts. Isolated, such a charism gradually becomes ideologized; either it is adopted for the whole, whereas it only constitutes a part, or the part is made an absolute and taken for the epitome of the Gospel. One may, of course, pitch one's tent somewhere near the center of the Gospel and emblazon love upon one's banner. But what applies to the Church applies to this charismatic love as well: it needs a structure in order to be truly part of the Church; otherwise it runs the risk of evaporating into something formless and vague. There are other charisms which define themselves according to a certain "principle" that is central to revelation, but the word alone shows the danger of making something personal—for example, the Holy Spirit or Mary—into something abstract and conceptual. The Holy Spirit is present only when he assuredly leads to Christ, even to the Cross. Mary in no way desires to be made the center of theology; she is both queen and handmaid, queen because she is handmaid. And if certain ancient orders have still failed to regain their identity, new movements and institutes must all the more reside in the center and let their center expand into the Church. Some do attempt this, and it is for this reason that one perceives in them little of the anti-Roman attitude.

Angelo Scola: But is not Rome the greatest obstacle for a fruitful ecumenical dialogue?

Hans Urs von Balthasar: Paul VI expressed this very clearly. What remains most difficult in the dialogue with other Christian denominations is that which has been expressly defined at the First Vatican Council. Strangely enough, it is the papacy which provides the decisive basis for any such dialogue. Why? Because it is only in the Catholic Church that we find a central point toward which one can orient oneself about the meaning of the word "catholic". If you talk to a Protestant, Anglican or an Orthodox Christian, there is usually one specific person or group with whom one can possibly reach an understanding. But another group of the same denomination will immediately object on the grounds that the decisive factor lies elsewhere. The reconciliation with Patriarch Athenagoras was a magnificent and moving episode, but in the face of dissension on the part of other Orthodox representatives, it must remain an episode. Catholics alone possess the advantage of having a true reference point, a center of ecclesiastical unity, willed by Christ himself. If we destroy it, we not only destroy the Church, but we also deprive ecumenism of its only chance for success. This, of course, does not imply that one should elevate the pope above the Church, as it is done in a quite incomprehensible and utterly untheological fashion by a party which dares call itself "The Movement for Pope and Church". They put the cart before the horse. They should call themselves: "The Movement for Judging the Pope and the Church".

Angelo Scola: Another significant issue is catechesis. How do you assess its future?

Hans Urs von Balthasar: As I am not a catechist, I have little to say. First of all, a general rule: a successful catechesis depends primarily on the person who communicates it and on the credible impression made upon the audience. One may ask at this point the serious and far-reaching question:

matic and a practical-ethical section; the latter should possess the required firmness and clarity as well as the necessary flexibility, for an overly-rigid approach may not always apply to the diversity of cultural traditions. And since Catholic Christians must not pass off the evangelical counsels of Christ concerning ethical conduct as "natural law", to be obeyed by all men, there emerges within the catechetical issue a much more sensitive question: Are identical norms to be applied to the devout as well as to the lukewarm? To those at the center of the Church and at the periphery?

No catechism can ever compress into a rigid system the Commands of Christ which always require a free response. We have a regrettable instance of this in the criticism which the head of "The Movement for Pope and Church" made of the catechism for adults, revised by Walter Kasper [English edition: *The Church's Confession of Faith*]. This text had been sanctioned by the entire body of German bishops, and carefully examined and corrected in part by representatives of several congregations in Rome. In one of these periodicals —which seem to have a franchise on ecclesiastical infallibility, sit in judgment on the whole Church and deal in heaven, hell and a patchwork of mysticism true and false—we may read this (against the authority of Rome and the German bishops' conference): "This catechism", it says, "leaves everything open to questioning, and instead of strengthening the faith, it has abandoned the paths of traditional theology." Why? "Because the *regula proxima* of faith is situated to a higher degree in the magisterial declarations of the popes and councils than in the Bible." Thus spoke Mr. X. Y., Pastor, presiding councillor of "The Movement for Pope and Church". It is good to be told so precisely with what yardsticks Christian revelation is measured.

Conciliar formulations are not to be abolished, but their declarations may be placed into new contexts. Everybody is familiar with the examples of Ephesus and Chalcedon, and there exist many others. Encyclicals are indeed normative, not, however, infallible. One could hardly deny that such a solidly-based, but in its wording not infallible, text as *Humanae Vitae* has unintentionally had a part in the collapse of the Church's practice of confession. An ecclesiastical text is authentic to the degree in which it approaches the distinctive mark of the biblical injunction: to be "spirit and life" and to animate both. (Cf. *Dei Verbum*, no. 21.)

Angelo Scola: Don't you think that the difficulty in producing good catechetical texts indicates how difficult the relationship between theology and Magisterium is?

Hans Urs von Balthasar: One ought not to exaggerate this difficulty which, incidentally, differs considerably from country to country. In the United States one has arrived at a stalemate, and to such a degree that Msgr. Kelly could name his substantial book, written with great conviction, *The Battle for the American Church*. At meetings between bishops and theologians one could not get beyond the point where the latter said to the bishops: your competence extends to this point (for example, to preach) and from there on ours begins (to inquire intelligently). With this theory of two teaching offices, nothing could of course be achieved, and one invariably reached the same impasse. The secretary of the bishops' conference had the good idea of inviting a few European theologians for a dialogue, which then suddenly and happily broke the ice. A living theology, rooted in the Bible, found an interested audience among the bishops, and a fruitful dialogue confirmed that theologians work for the prophetic Church, while the episcopate welcomes an effective examination of crucial scriptural texts. In other countries the situation may be quite different. In Germany, for instance, a number of eminent theologians—beginning in our generation with Cardinal Volk—have been appointed bishops.

In general it may be said—and both catechists and preachers should exercise the appropriate discernment here—that the results, especially of exegetical inquiry, are valid on substantially very different levels. There are those which are indisputable and evident, and they should be reported to the faithful with the necessary prudence; others again, and they are numerous, are but scientific hypotheses, which may change with the successive generations of exegetes and may even turn into their opposite: to speak of these to the people in catechisms or in sermons is irresponsible, although this is repeatedly done by an exegetically half-educated clergy. It can only cause scandal and may frequently lead to loss of faith.

Angelo Scola: In his long interview, Cardinal de Lubac said, among other things, that the phrase *instauratio et progressio* could serve as a motto for the coming synod of bishops.

Hans Urs von Balthasar: Instauratio, or as has been said, *restauratio*, is certainly a concept to be handled with care. Both these words can only be employed in referring to matters of the past. We, however, should always be mindful of the ever-present Christ and his Spirit as he is with us today in the Church. The issue is not one of going back two thousand years in order to become, in Kierkegaard's sense, "simultaneous" with Christ. His promise, to be with us unto the end of time, assures us of his simultaneity, particularly if we keep our faith alive. It is true, of course, that this faith of ours may always be awakened from its sleep and restored to the truth, so that it may be alive with the living Christ in the Church. The Church, too, which is Christ's Body, is constantly admonished to be conformed to the Head.

How can one "progress" if one stands already in the end-time? The Church is eschatological, even while she is still a pilgrim in this world. The *pleroma* of Christ as her head has been given to her, Saint Paul says (Eph 4:13), so that she may grow to the fullness of her age. This growth within the *pleroma* to which she has been called can only signify that Christians must become increasingly aware of the fullness already received, remember perhaps certain aspects of this plenitude, which have been forgotten over the centuries or in their own lifetime. In this respect Catholics may learn much—why not—from Protestant and Orthodox Christians, or from Muslims, who may have retained some things fresher in their memory and demonstrated them in their personal lives. Furthermore, *progressio* is highly significant when applied to holiness. Here Saint Paul speaks of a perpetual movement which never comes to a stand-still, not a measuring of what has already been achieved: "Not that I have already obtained this, or already have been made perfect, but I press on, hoping that I may lay hold of that for which Jesus has laid hold of me" (Phil 3:12). Holiness is not assembled in a workshop; the saints are gifts from God, and they remain so; also, when God sends the Church new saints, the old ones do not become dated because of it. And not one of them ever thought of himself as holy or canonized himself; all of them were on the way, *in progressione*, even the Mother of the Lord. Only in that sense should the Church progress—but in a manner entirely different from that of the world, of history, culture and technology. Of course, the Church is left with the often burdensome task of having to establish guidelines, corresponding to revelation. She must do this vis-à-vis the current situation, which is characterized by economic and political problems and, above all, by a rapidly developing technology. These guidelines, however, can never be reduced to the same level as the world's problems themselves: they would inevitably be caught up in a temporal and hence replaceable casuistry. They are rather to sustain that spiritual height from which Christians receive the call to make free and responsible decisions in response to the demands made by God in Christ. Christian teachings only apparently develop on this level; what develops are the world's problems (one thinks of the pill, genetic manipulation, means of total warfare, and so forth), in the face of which the immutable and hence unsurpassable Gospel may well be challenged by new questions and be exposed to a new, worldly light. The Gospel message, however, is not changed by this process, although the Church cannot derive

77

On Sexuality and Hope

Angelo Scola: I had to occupy myself extensively with the teaching of our present Holy Father concerning love and its physical expression. In my first course on the subject, I developed a theology of man's original state, which is closely related to the one you developed in your book, *The Christian State of Life*. How do you assess this aspect of the Holy Father's teaching authority?

Hans Urs von Balthasar: A distinction should be drawn between the extraordinary personality of our Pope, who is a philosopher and a spiritual theologian, and the *munus magisterii*. After all, we could have an entirely different pope, who might not be a philosopher, and yet could state the tenets of our faith in quite a simple manner. To what degree is the personal philosophy and theology of the Holy Father authoritative for the universal Church? I think his teachings expressly contain theses which are central to the understanding of our faith: the body, for instance, the human person, the community and the wonderful things he has to say on human labor and divine mercy. What is developed here is rooted directly in revelation, and should be pondered by every Christian, not in order to construct a closed system with his encyclicals, but to obtain from his great intuitions a point of departure from which new reflections on divine revelations may emerge. I consider his thoughts concerning the body of the highest importance, because the subject has always been, and still is, surrounded by forms of Platonism and spiritualism, which disparage the body and everything material in favor of a pure spirituality. It may be said that all types of non-Christian meditation, most of all the Eastern ones, force the meditator to leave behind all that is corporal, even the imagination and concrete concepts. They do this in crass opposition to the doctrine of the Incarnation of God in Christ: everything spiritual in God should become incarnate—and remain so even to the resurrection of the body.

Angelo Scola: The press in several countries have taken up an interview you gave to the *Nouvel Observateur*, in which you spoke, among other things, of the role of sexuality in contemporary society. Can you repeat the essential points?

Hans Urs von Balthasar: The concept of transcending the bodily sphere is unknown in the New Testament. But the way in which a person lives his bodily life involves, especially nowadays, a great deal of disorder. We Christians cannot, as we have said before, force our respective norms upon an atheistic society, but we can exemplify an approxi-

our bodies at the disposal of Christ, just as he, too, surrendered his whole body to the Church. The Eucharist is certainly situated on a higher plane than marriage, which, according to Saint Paul, is meant to be an image of the unity between Christ and the Church. But the Church, too, is a bodily reality and not an abstraction; neither is she a mere collective (as "people"), nor just the sum of particular members ("particular" churches), but already in Mary a truly organic-corporeal entity. Mary is Mother, and brings forth the Son of God from her own body. Her motherhood is so fundamental and irrevocable that her crucified Son makes her on the one hand the mother of the beloved disciple, and therewith Mother of the Church, and on the other, because of this, his spouse. In both respects Mary is the center of the Church, which is designated *immaculata* (Eph 5:27): the Church is that perfectly only in her. To recapitulate: the Church is no abstract entity; only real, corporeal persons participate in her. They are ecclesial to the degree in which their personal mission—Origen speaks of an *anima ecclesiastica*—their charism, extends into the reality of the universal Church, as happens in the case of prayer, for instance, or of suffering. In an essay entitled *"Who is the Church?"* (which Fr. Congar said he did not understand) I express the view that the ecclesial radiance of a person extends as far as his (accomplished) mission. Seen from that angle, Mary's mission radiates throughout the whole Church (the image of the "protective mantle" expresses this symbolically), and analogous to this, other charisms radiate across vast spaces of the Church. Remember Saint Francis, who not only radiates throughout the orders which live from his mission, but beyond that, all "franciscan" souls. Saint Francis is not an idea but a reality.

Angelo Scola: If you had to write your little book *Love Alone* over again, what would you wish to add?

Hans Urs von Balthasar: I suppose some clarifying remarks. Essentially, I merely wished to show that God's truth and justice do not exist outside of his love. The notion that God's "attributes" can be separated from each other is incorrect. Such separations only exist within the categorical order of substance and accidents; being, however, and even more so God, transcend this order. For if it can be said that the transcendentals—being, oneness, truth, goodness, beauty—penetrate each other indivisibly, how much more can this be said of God's attributes. Saint Anselm understood this when he deduced God's goodness and mercy on the one hand and his justice on the other from a common source, namely, God's *rectitude*: everything God is and does is right. Saint Thomas goes one step further when he declares that the whole of creation owes its existence exclusively to God's pure goodness; his justice (as a form of his goodness) only comes into play once the world existed. It is indeed true to say that God in his wisdom must create all things in a manner befitting their nature (for instance, he endows man with hands, so that he can work); this justice God owes to his creatures. But then Saint Thomas quickly adds: more profoundly, God owes this justice only to himself, to his ineffable goodness, so that no creature may make any demand whatsoever on God ("You owe it to me, to give me this or that"). Always it is God's goodness that judges with justice. And God's freedom manifests itself, according to Saint Thomas, by the fact that he always gives more than mere justice demands: God's mercy, by his power to forever heal the deficiencies and errors of his creatures. In the Old as well as in the New Covenant, this divine mercy takes first place.

Angelo Scola: This is the fundamental idea of the *Satin Slipper* by Claudel. Do you know, by the way, that it was the object of a film that lasted six hours?

Hans Urs von Balthasar: No. But I saw a complete performance in Paris, which also took six hours. It played to a full house for I don't know how many performances. Hope must be seen as a theological virtue (*espérance* is more than *espoir*), which is an expectation oriented toward God. There is no such thing as an earthly *espérance*, at best an *espoir*, an expectation that "hopefully" things will turn out well, that the world as a whole will perhaps become better. To place human and theological hope on an equal plane might be one of the dangers of liberation theology. Saint Bonaventure calls theological hope, by which we desire the divine good, infallible; according to him one may say that I can always hope for the best from God, which I shall receive, if I persevere in hope. If I lose hope, I lose at the same time its infallibility. If I retain it, I will infallibly receive what I had hoped for. Thus the Lord promises: "Whatever you ask in my name (meaning, in my sense), that you shall receive" (Mk 11:24) and the First Letter of Saint John: "When we know that God listens to our prayer, we know that we already possess what we prayed for" (1 Jn 5:15).

Angelo Scola: What relationship do you see between hope and final salvation?

Hans Urs von Balthasar: I am presently engaged in a confrontation with the German "right", which insists at all costs that one may not hope for the salvation of all men, since there exists full certainty that some will be damned. Such a certainty appears to me unwarranted. For one, the Church has never asserted any man's damnation, and there are numerous New Testament texts pointing in the opposite direction: "God wills all men to be saved", and "If I be lifted up, I will draw all things to myself." There are many such texts. Thus hope for all men seems to be permitted, as long as one does not seek to anticipate the judgment of the Lord, or preach a theory of universal salvation. But the gesture of Christ in Michelangelo's *Last Judgment* seems to me theologically inappropriate.

Angelo Scola: Will you deal with this subject in *Theo-Drama*?

Hans Urs von Balthasar: In connection with soteriology, yes. It is necessary to come to terms with Moltmann's concept of hope, also with Bloch's and others. I should like to conclude with an eschatology which will know as its last thing (*eschaton*) not the destiny of man but the Blessed Trinity. The last thing is not "my" death, "my" judgment, but God as the concluding horizon of all. This section is, incidentally, finished. What lies ahead is the last wing of my triptych which deals with "theologic".

Angelo Scola: And what is this about?

Hans Urs von Balthasar: It is about divine truth. More precisely, how the invariably trinitarian truth can be translated into an apparently dual human truth (something is either true or false). There is, however, no such dual logic, as Hegel has well understood, though we do not have to become Hegelians because of it. The Cross of Christ, the "speculative Friday" of Hegelian dialectic, remains, whatever one may say, abstract. Christ, however, is concrete. So is the family: man, woman and child. I went through the images of the Trinity as they appear in creation to gain a basis from which to explain how Christ could translate the divine trinitarian message into human language and reality, which is always trinitarian. I am only suggesting here what needs to be carefully developed.

In the end there remains a final task for logic to perform. The Word of God first speaks, then suffers, dies and rises in the end. Only the three syllables together make up the whole Word, which God addresses to us in Christ. The first syllable by itself could not be comprehended by the disciples. The whole becomes comprehensible only with the coming of the Holy Spirit into the heart. It must be demonstrated that the Holy Spirit, as the revealed love of the Father in the Incarnate Son, can explain to us what God is. Fr. Ignace de la Potterie may be right in showing that "truth" in Saint John is nothing but the presentation of the Father's divine love in the human appearance of Christ. Before Pilate, who is his judge, he says: "I have come to bear witness to the truth." What the

sideration but a new access to the center. Before Augustine, many had spoken of the love of God, but none did it in as penetrating a manner as he. Before Ignatius, no one had grasped Christ's obedience to the Father in quite so central a way. Correspondingly, aspects exist in Adrienne's work that have not been as expressly discovered in revelation before her. But once examined carefully, one realizes that they "work". A case in point is her reflection on prayer in the triune God: prayer not only, as one had always understood, as something that ascends from man to God, but, more profoundly, what descends from God to man, permitting a participation in the inner-trinitarian prayer of God. In God himself lie the archetypes of all our modes of prayer. Within the trinitarian life God worships God, God may petition God; in thanksgiving one may recognize how the One God, within the Trinity, can make a choice, form a decision. The Holy Spirit, who is poured into our hearts, who searches the depth of God, is given to us too, elevating us into the sphere of inner-trinitarian prayer. This is but one of many instances in which Adrienne first astonishes, and then, on further reflection, brings joy. I believe the Church will gradually have to adopt substantial parts of her doctrine and, perhaps, wonder why these beautiful and enriching things have not been recognized earlier. But the Holy Spirit distributes his gifts when he wills. And we may come to

entrance into the clerical profession, on their terms, which the Church is not able to accept. On the other side we see those positions which can be filled only by laymen—positions of the highest importance for the Church—practically deserted. The first group shows an understandable exasperation when, after impetuously knocking at the clerical door and trying to force it open with irrefutable arguments ("They will need us in the end"), their demands are not met. (There is not only an anti-Roman but also an anti-clerical attitude displayed by those who wish to force their way into the clergy.) On the other side, we find it virtually impossible to obtain able young Catholic journalists, writers, publishers and other professionals. No doubt, lay-theologians who could not succeed in that field find a refuge in such positions, but it is questionable whether they achieve their professional goals, just as it is questionable whether some of them should not have become priests in the first place, as the Church in her wisdom desires.

I know, my dear friend, that conditions in your country are entirely different from ours, but I cannot help being newly astonished whenever I look at your situation in Italy. Unless I am completely mistaken, it is the members of the ecclesiastical movements who particularly excel in the secular professions. They are the ones who have created such astonishing things as the weeklies and monthlies published under your auspices, a pub-

alone appears to them worthy of faith, commitment and proclamation. To put it negatively: matters which cannot be embraced in prayer are not worthy to be thought of, and even less to be preached. Thus they have arrived at a good criterion for what theology really is, without falling into a moralizing or, worse still, politicizing pragmatism. Theologies which have been invented in 1968 or later as a *dernier cri* of modernity are no longer of interest to them, and the same holds true of any narrow-minded conservatism. For these young priests revelation is alive in the Church today, as it was from the beginning the language and gift of the living God and not a museum of frozen formulas. "The truth shall make you free", says the Lord. He and his disciples were not given to lengthy deliberations on what their audience might be inclined to hear or accept. "Teach them to keep what I have taught you", not simply what you think they are capable of. Such things may indeed be appropriate, but, due to their selection, they will lack credibility. Only when the body of revelation does not lack a single member is it whole. Then it will not be in need of artificial members. Its wholeness speaks for itself. Do you understand now that a healthy young generation of future priests desires nothing more than the *doctrina sana*, the sound doctrine of which the pastoral letters constantly speak?